Chanak Pai

CW00419029

Secrets to ~~Protect~~
Yourself from
Your Enemies Attack

PRIYANKA GULSHAN

Acknowledgement

In this book, an attempt has been made to translate
the words of Acharya Chanakya into simple words.
Any line or any sentence used in this book is a
verse spoken by Acharya Chanakya,
which has been explained in simple language.
And all those lines are being used appropriately to
educate people and to promote knowledge
related to the history of
our own country India .
I have only done translations in this book and
therefore I cannot take full credit for this book.
Rather,

The entire credit of this book
goes to Acharya Chanakya .
Because his words have guided all of us
till today and will continue to guide us forever .

In this book we will talk about
all those tricks and conspiracies
Which your enemy can use against you.

Acharya Chanakya
used these conspiracies and policies
only
And only
for the sake of goodness,
to build a united India .

That is why

I will request everyone
whoever gets this book

Do not recommend reading this book
to any such person
who you think
will use this book
for their bad purposes,

This is your responsibility .

Read these policies
very carefully
And
use them only for good work .

A disciple pays tribute to
Acharya Chanakya

Tvam-Eva Maataa
-Cha Pitaa Tvam-Eva

Tvam-Eva Bandhush
-Cha Sakhaa Tvam-Eva

Tvam-Eva Viidyaa
Dravinnam Tvam-Eva

Tvam-Eva Sarvam
Mama Deva Deva

Meaning -

You Truly are my Mother And You
Truly are my Father .
You Truly are my Relative And You
Truly are my Friend.
You Truly are my Knowledge and You
Truly are my Wealth.
You Truly are my All, My God of Gods.

कखगघङ
चछजझञ
टठडढण
तथदधन

FIRST NEETI

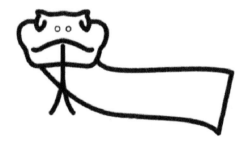

शषसह
यरलव
पफबभम

EXPLAIN-
BUY-
PUNISH-
REVEAL !

Explain -
by explaining One can get his/her
work done, by making others
believe how important your work is
and why it is needed to be done

Buy -
getting the work done
by the power of your Money

Punish -
To punish the person who is wrong
for his bad deeds so that they don't
repeat the same mistakes again

Reveal -
Knowing one's secrets
and using their secrets against them
to create divisions among their
people to break their unity

EXPLAIN-BUY-PUNISH-REVEAL-

+

FEED-FEAR-SLEEP

Looking at the modern era, these policies are correct But apart from these, some other things can also be noticed. That is, instead of bringing changes in these policies, some more things can be added to these policies.
{ Feed - Fear - Sleep }
I am adding some things to it from my side. I hope that you will accept all these changes.

Feed -
that is, when the work is not done by paying the price, then feed the person with some food, win his heart and get your work done

Fear -
Whatever they fear, use it !
that is, get your work done out of fear, out of superstition.

And

Sleep -
That means make your opponent lazy
Now you will ask that
how is that possible ?

For example -

Hire your opponent for some money.
And instead of giving them work to
do, tell them to sit all day and read
newspaper or watch television.
That is pay them and ask them to do
nothing . And do this for a few
months and then fire them .
And then you will notice yourself
that how your opponent will lose his
ability to work .

Such a person who is struck by
laziness will never be able to
achieve success again.
{ unless and until they try with
their will-power. }

कखगघङ

चछजझञ

टठडढण

तथदधन

SECOND NEETI

शषसह

यरलव

पफबभम

The battle is won
not by force
but by intelligence.

Therefore,
first find out the
shortcomings
of your enemy.

Then strike there ,
where by attacking
He will suffer
the most injuries.

In this verse, Acharya Chanakya says that -
War does not only require force.
Because one can also win by wisdom only.

If the force you have, if it is not used
with the right intelligence, with the right tact,
that is, if you don't use your intelligence
to create a proper chakravyuh.
{ proper attacking strategy }
Then that force
is completely useless.

That is why a person should first find out
the shortcomings of his enemy
before landing in the battlefield
and try to make his shortcomings his strength, one
should find his own flaws and do not repeat
Their mistakes again and one should try to make
themselves more powerful and capable.
Before planning and facing his enemies,
Firstly a person should pay more attention to the
weaknesses of his enemy and make those
weaknesses of his enemy his goal.
And strike where he suffers the most by attacking
him on his weak points
in simple words, make your enemy's weaknesses
your strengths.

Because It is his arrogance that he thinks that - it is
not my weakness but only a small ignorable point
and how my enemy will possibly spoil me with
this minor defect, it is the arrogance of that person
which makes him more inattentive and careless

he doesn't allow the truth to be seen by himself .
And this foolishness of your enemy
will be your strong point
And will prove to be the advantage
that you want the most .

Therefore, do not consider any of your mistakes
as small, keep a far-sighted thought ,
think about your weak points
and how your enemy can use them against you and
will plot in which ways to break you ?
Never think that your enemy won't notice your
weaknesses , because they will !
They will watch you , monitor you , consider your
every move and will stake their everything
only to defeat you and so
you must not be the reason for your own defeat !

And in order to do so make sure
not to cover your weaknesses but to remove them
from the roots of their existence !

Improve yourself , work on your weaknesses
in such a way that they become your strengths,
Surprise your enemy with your improvement ,
break his confidence that he will never be able to
defeat you because you will keep changing .

Remedy in a sentence -

Work on your shortcomings
instead of hiding them from yourself,
finish them completely.

क ख ग घ ङ
च छ ज झ ञ
ट ठ ड ढ ण
त थ द ध न

THIRD NEETI

श ष स ह
य र ल व
प फ ब भ म

Only those will change the history who will Dare to Dream !

Divide And rule !

This is the only rule in politics.

Politics means getting your work done
out of crookedness
and this can be possible
only when human beings create
divisions among the people.

That is, if there is a debate or any atmosphere of
tension, then even the possibility of that debate
should not be left, that is
one should
Lit the fire where there is oil,
One spark would be enough to advance that debate
or that tension in that group,

It often happens that in any big party,
small groups are formed. And those groups have
their own separate leaders. And where there will be
many groups, there will definitely be
misunderstandings and differences along with
different kinds of thoughts.

Now when such different ideas come close to each
other, then their are chances of a big fight with the
increasing tension and pressure, disobeying,
betrayal and loud voices even from one side may
lead to a big miss,

And the moment the two factions clashes wholly ,
that moment, every person, the entire structure of
that group will disintegrate.

And at the same time, the opposing party who was
sitting ambush will then attack on them in a way

that their party will never be able to unite again
Because of there own difference, their own fights
this house of cards will shatter when their house
will be on fire from inside and from outside !

Remedy in a few sentences -

That is why when small groups and even good
people are working together, they should also
understand that there is strength in unity.
At any time, the moment when anyone will
manage to get a split in their mindset. And the
moment this seed of suspicion arise in their mind,
they will fight with each other
Until they get divided into fraction and get
destroyed, that is why you should always try to
keep unity in your party and should keep all the
small differences aside.
Try to solve them. And find the cause as to who
developed these differences, were they a part of
your enemies plan or was it just jealously

Be it anything
if differences are hidden
or even if they are shown,
if they live
then your unity won't !
Destroy the spark before It lit's the fire
Or get ready to collect the ashes for which
your enemy desire !

कखगघङ
चछजझञ
टठडढण
तथदधन

FOURTH NEETI

शषसह
यरलव
पफबभम

Whenever, suddenly if
things go one by one
before us more
than expected,
If there are
coincidences,
Again and again,
then understand,
that something is going
on inappropriately.

What is a coincidence ?
Is that the only sign of luck
that everything is going right in your life ?

No !

This is a coincidence, its not necessary,
has it just arisen on its own ?
What do you think ?
Things just don't happens by themselves
Until and unless there is someone playing with
your stack of cards !
It can also be possible that some person is
Manipulating your decisions in a way that even
you don't know it yet , or maybe you do , you just
have not seen it carefully
Maybe they are creating an impression of these
coincidence to trap you in their trap.
Hiding somewhere, watching it all,
just waiting to trap you in !
Small coincidence are enough to take you in one
direction, enough to confuse you.
Therefore, a human being should look carefully at
every event that happens in his life.
Were those incidents very simple ?
were there some moments in your life that looked
very easy and unlikely ?
What circumstances were taking you in those
directions, and do you really wanted to go there
where you went ?
In the direction from where you have reached here
today.

Think for yourself if there was ever a real chance that all things will become very simple and easy and every event will turn your path towards ease ? Can that ever really happen ? Or are you just making yourself believe that it is happening ? Simplicity is only an illusion, which is laid out by someone else, nothing is simple, but it can be made simple and what makes it simple may not be necessarily good towards you. Maybe they are simplifying your route because they know that by going ahead on this path you will have to face a lot of difficulties and you will not have the ability or the courage to face them. Or in a simple way, this simple route can also be a plot against you. Be careful and think at every step of your life. Whatever is happening. Do not forget it, remember it, so that you can go ahead and understand whether all this was destiny or was it happening to everyone or was it someone's creation ?

Remedy in a few sentences -

When only the path of ease and simplicity starts to appear in your entire life, then understand that there is some wrong, scam going on somewhere. Maybe someone is weaving a trap for you and Waiting for you to step into it and to get trapped But right now you do not know that. But by watching your circumstances carefully, you will definitely understand these tricksters. The most simplest path will always lead a man astray. Always Do remember this thing !

कखगघङ
चछजझञ
टठडढण
तथदधन

FIFTH NEETI

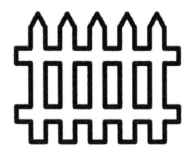

शषसह
यरलव
पफबभम

**If you cannot
control the king.
So control the person,
The One
who can control
the thoughts
of the king.**

We want to control the king so that whatever
decision the king makes is favourable to us.
But in many situations, it is possible that the king
may also show favouritism. And if they do not act
on our advice, and don't do the needed right, then
Acharya Chanakya has said that When we are not
able to control the king, then we should put our
control on the person who determines
the thoughts of the king
because if such a person will join us, then with his
help we will be able to show the king the right path
which will save the kingdom.

Many times it happens that the decisions of the
king are not only for his subjects but also are
influenced by the greed of the rest of the states, he
can also takes some difficult decisions, but the
people who live near him who can influence his
thinking They have the ability to change his
decisions. They have the ability to correct his
decisions and explain to the him what is right and
is needed to be done.

But now you will ask
how can someone completely change the thinking
ability of the king, who is close to the king,
who can change the thinking of the king.
How does this happen ?

Whichever person is closest / near to the king.
They will have some effect on the heart and mind
of the king. People usually say that the personality
of a human being is determined by the people

living around them. How the behaviour of a human being will be determined by the fact that he lives in association with which people, how will this happen and why , it happens because the effect of association is very much on the life of a human being. Whether you believe it or not
The compatibility of a human being can also change him, can also ride him and can also put him in trouble.
In exactly the same manner as a person living near the king, can bend, break and change his ideologies. When such a person can change the king's ideologies for a good cause. In exactly the same way, if that same person meets with a bad person, then he can also give a wrong direction to the thinking of the king. No matter how good the king is, When we are close to someone, we trust them blindly and won't see good and evil, in our own decisions just because the people around us told us to do so we will do it if we really trust them
Without considering the slightest possibility of them being wrong When the king is near his own people, this trust will shadow his mind and his decisions, he won't question their thoughts he will think - How can they be wrong, they will choose the right path only, because they care for me !
Right ? Wrong ! Maybe they just pretend they do and they never did ! It is a fight of the heart and the mind that does not let us see the right and the wrong. Due to this confusion, we always consider our loved ones as being right. So no matter who you are. Whether a king or not you will be influenced by the people you love the most !

When the decision of the king can change. Your's can too ? Still No ? Why ? which field's radish are you ? Jokes aside ! Your thoughts can also be changed and it may also happen that you are not aware that someone is changing your thoughts. And the friend who is changing your thoughts may not even know as to who changed his thoughts ? That seed of doubt, maybe all that it took was that only ! To change your friends decisions to change them to change you, maybe some third person has created this doubt in your friend's mind. But you will eventually make a wrong decision, because of this influence which you probably would not have take if your friend wouldn't have sown that seed of doubt in your mind.

Remedy in a few lines -
choose your associates and friends wisely. Those who do not want good for you, They not only know your about your weak points but they also know your friends who can be turned from your asset into your biggest weaknesses
they also know whether you get affected quickly or not. You will find many people who will stab you in the back. But we have to learn to handle ourselves carefully. It is not possible now for you to depend on someone else, so whatever decision you make, Think about it carefully that are you taking those decisions by being influenced by someone else ? Are these decisions really your own ? Question everything ! Even the things you think you already know !

क ख ग घ ङ
च छ ज झ ञ
ट ठ ड ढ ण
त थ द ध न

SIXTH NEETI

श ष स ह
य र ल व
प फ ब भ म

There is power
in power.
Which can make
others obedient !
And those who have
authority,
Can giving orders
to anyone.
They Can force
anyone to listen.

There is power in power,
that is, who possesses power,
who possesses force,
who possesses wealth and money.
He can get his work done
by getting anyone to do anything,
by giving them sufficient amount of money.
Whether it is wrong or right.
Even today, there is so much power in power
that any member of any one group will agree to go
against their own, only for power.
Without even thinking what will be its adverse
effects and whether they are doing right or wrong ?

Man can try to change,
but cannot change his destiny,
greed, money, hunger or poverty can compels a
human being to do such work which maybe
against the human nature
But this is the truth of this world.

Money - Strength - Power

These are the 3 things
that can make a person do anything !
Lot of money or
Enormous strength or even a powerful position !
If anyone has Even One of these things
then he can deposit more money.
And If all these three are owned by one person
then that person will have the ability to make
people dance at his fingertips !

Remedy in a few sentences -

That is why a person needs to be so capable, that he can do his work on his own. And even if he could not do his own work, then he should be able to earn so much money by doing the right thing that he could get his work done by the people.

But for this too, not only strength will be required but intelligence will also have to be used and maybe vicious work will also have to be done. Because maybe when you think of doing something good with your money, strength or power, then someone else who has the same money, strength and power, may create obstacles or challenges in your path because it may be due to your decisions which you are going to take which may lead to bad people's downfall or simply they can just create obstacles in your path just because of jealousy.

That is why money should not become heedless even after gaining strength and power. And be sure to pay attention to all the events happening around you.
When power,
strength
and money
can be given
They can also be snatched easily away
Be capable on your own !
And stay away from greed !

कखगघङ
चछजझञ
टठडढण
तथदधन

SEVENTH NEETI

शषसह
यरलव
पफबभम

The most valuable
assets in the War
Are the Secrets and
Information of your
Enemy's side !
They can tell us a lot.
And when we get them
So they does not only
give us strength but
they also give us the
base to act upon !

The Secrets and all the information
of the enemy's side
can tell us about our enemy's thinking.
They can tell about their next conspiracies and
their tricks. They can warns us,
Regarding what the enemy's next move will be,
So that we will be able to
prepare for our counter move.

It is very important to know your enemy,
understand him, and to practice
his conspiracies beforehand.
If we get to know about all these things of the
opposition in advance,
then victory is sure to happen.

But who will give you this information?

Secret variables !

Placed Spies !

Someone who can work for us
with our enemy.
A person who makes such a distinction,
who combines with the enemy so well as if
he's on the enemy's side.
Someone Who would gain the trust of our enemy
to be with them to learn their secrets .
But make sure that they are with you
from their heart.
But as every problem is always solved
Sometimes solutions can be harmful too.

Who knows ?
Maybe some day your own spy will start working
for the opposition and may tell you some wrong
information about your enemy,
stuff that your enemy wants you to hear.
So you have to be careful about your own policies,
you must not let them leak, do not tell your
policies, plans and your next moves in-front of
anyone even in-front of your own spy.
Why ?
Because your information is valuable too
And other can always tricks you before you trick
them, Always remember that !
Use your intelligence only to get the required
information and remember not to give any
personal or business information about yourself or
your own group.

Remedy in a few sentences -

Make use of as much information
as you can from your enemy's side,
But even if you have hired any detective,
do not trust him completely.
Always Keeping this in mind,
Make your strategies
but do not wholly depend on them !
Because even your detective can cheat you.
Betray you !
Create many policies, don't just focus your plan on
a single thing be read for the worse
even when you are winning !

क ख ग घ ङ
च छ ज झ ञ
ट ठ ड ढ ण
त थ द ध न

EIGHTH NEETI

श ष स ह
य र ल व
प फ ब भ म

**Keep going
as per the tricks of
your enemy,
Until they feel
confident that you
have been deceived
by their tricks.
And when your enemy
becomes inattentive,
then trick them into
their own tricks
and beat them.**

By following our enemy's tricks, our enemy will get this illusion that we are trapped in his trap. They will Think that we are following his strategies but our enemy will never know this, that we are already many steps ahead of him, recognising and moving forward in his strategies And tricks because we know what is going to happen next and we can manipulate the outcome ! By doing this, when we fall into our enemies trap then our enemy will become inattentive and then somewhere in their arrogance, They will start thinking that they are about to win Our move in that moment will determine our fate either we will fall deeper into our enemies trap or we will be able to recover and make a move much to our enemies surprise ! At that time, either we will get entangled in our enemies trick very badly or we will be able to beat our enemy, by throwing new tricks on them. Our goal should not only be focused on our strengths but also on the weakness of our enemy that whenever we get a change and see their guards down, then be ready to fight with your weapons ! And that ambush will prove to be the most beneficial for us, because our enemy will not be alert at that time, they will not even know about that ambush and they would be so surprise that they will make more mistakes in haste! And will get slowly closer to their own defeat. Because it doesn't matter how the victory was won ? Or how long it took, The world will only remember those who won.

Whether they get the victory in 5 minutes by
cleverness or by using force, they can fight for
years or more but that's not the goal, the real goal
is to win, by whatever means necessary
to establish the good back in the world !
But it can also happen that when we are going
deep in our enemy's trick, our detective can also
tell all our secrets to our enemy
And so we must be prepared for that as well !
By any means, through the help of the detective we
have hired or by any possible way, if our enemy
will get the slightest of the hint that we already
know their next move, then their situation of
alertness can bring a lot of trouble for us !
They will become careful and cautions of us
And they may entangled us further in their trap
until we accept our defeat !

Remedy in a few sentences -

Know the enemy, his tricks and then pretend to be
falling for them but always remember situations
can change anytime, people from your side can
also betray ! Trick them into thinking
that you are tricked but don't do that blindly
because that as well can be a trap of its own !
So take care and never let your secrets out
The most appropriately
kept secret
is the one
which you always keep,
only to yourself !

कखगघङ
चछजझञ
टठडढण
तथदधन

NINTH NEETI

शषसह
यरलव
पफबभम

The main five elements which
controls the art of war are -

Heaven or Fate.
Earth or Karma.
Commander.
Operation method.
And Discipline.

And above all,
The Most Important.
Moral rules !

Moral law is that rule.
which is the cause of
Influence and Belief.
The subjects are
restricted to their king.

There is such a moral trap
In which you can get the public
to do whatever you want.
You can confuse the public with
this morality !
in the web of hope,
While in reality there will be no
hope ! With the help of this
moral trap, despite of the
public's lack of hope,
You can assure them
that there is hope.
In this way you can encourage
their self-respect.
You can revive their life.
In a way That even after having
other options for themselves
They will be ready to sacrifice
their life for you.

Fate - means luck
Karma - that is, good or bad deeds
of a human beings
If he does good work then he will get good fruit.
Destiny will give bad results to those who do bad
things.
Commander - will show the direction
to your army.
Does he have so much strength, courage and
intelligence that he can show the right direction to
the whole army and keep them in sync.
To keep them united so that they can focus on their
original goal because if the commander becomes
useless, then the whole army will certainly
disintegrate.
Operation method - your strategies, they
Must be very good and
Discipline - is the rule which is very important.
And whoever does not follow this rule
will surely face defeat.
All these rules are very important, in any war,
it is very clear,
But the most important rule is
Moral rule
Moral law is a rule that is a trap.
One such false console.
By which people can be encouraged, they can be
shown dreams of hope even after disappointment.
Moral law works when one's goal is far greater
than one's own life and is for the benefit of
everyone or even when people are made to believe
that something will benefit them
and it is for their own good.

These rules work even if they are tricked by
claiming goodness even in the evil.
It's purpose may vary according to who is the
policy makes and what is his intent !
There will be many such times in your life when
people will try to entertain you, to be with you,
only to convince you to be in a war with someone.
Then how to find out whether we are drifting in
our friend's trap or should we really participate in
this war because it's really for the right reasons.
There is only one way to find out and that is
You only have to use your intelligence,
not your heart.
You have to think that is this war really needed ?
Or will this war only Serve the purpose of your
friend who is asking you to participate ?
Are people using you for their own purpose ?
Or is it really necessary ?
Measures in simple sentences -
A person should make a very thoughtful decision,
because nowadays, many people will meet you
only to deviate you from your path and
to make you fight for their bad cause.
They will go to any extent to fulfil their objective.
People should use their intelligence and do not get
involved in such fruitless battles which will not
benefit anyone. Before anyone comes under the
pretext of the fight, definitely think about it.
That will this battle harm our own land ?
And definitely think who is telling you to fight this
battle. Are these people who are suggesting you to
fight are these people really on the good side or do
they just pretend to be ?

क ख ग घ ङ
च छ ज झ ञ
ट ठ ड ढ ण
त थ द ध न

TENTH NEETI

श ष स ह
य र ल व
प फ ब भ म

**Always remember
one thing
The deadliest weapon
possessed by the ruler
in this game of politics
is his distinct
understanding and
his style of thinking.**

Distinct Thinking is the most
lethal weapon of the ruler
That how many policies he can think of without
missing any loose ends ?
How many remedies can he give
for a single problem ?
And will he be able to tell the solution as soon as
he hears the problem ?
This will depend on the thinking of that ruler that
whether he will be able to solve the
problems of life or not ?
The point of view of that ruler must also be very
correct. That is, the ruler must have foresight.
Otherwise, he will remain entangled
in the midst of small problems.
And the security of the state will be forgotten.
That is, by focusing on the basic issues, he will
become so busy in fighting with small difficulties
that he will forget that how much other issues,
such as state's security is necessary for him
as well as for his state.

Measures in simple sentences -

Man should think in every direction.
There can be many solutions, not just one solution
to a problem. Therefore, a human being
should keep a distant vision !
Don't just think about the problems which are
close to you right now. One should also think
about the problems which may arise in the later
life to come and you should be ready to fight with
those challenges as well.

क ख ग घ ङ
च छ ज झ ञ
ट ठ ड ढ ण
त थ द ध न

ELEVENTH NEETI

श ष स ह
य र ल व
प फ ब भ म

Even though
these people are not
listening to you today.
But
when they will
understand You
Then they
Will listen to you
and will also
accompany you.
You just have to wait
for the right time.

There are many times in life when we are right and still no one is listening to us. This happens because people don't recognise us then.
And they do not listen to us by considering us as someone who would know.
Whereas in your life as well you will see that for yourself that if there is anyone who is considered to be very well known. If he speaks anything. Even if it is nonsense, people will still listen to them very carefully.
This is the only law of life.
That people like to listen to the people whom they know or at least whom they think they know, people who are famous and are considered important we do also listen to them. Don't we ? Without even considering the possibility that this famous person can be stupid as hell ! Wether it is right or wrong, people will support their decision.
Some people are also of the opinion that, that person must have reached the heights in his life because he must have done good things. That is not necessary as well ! This is a biggest mistake of people of misunderstanding those who they think or pretend to know ! You must stand on what you think is right. Do not change your ideologies because of anyone, only think and understand what you think, not what others are forcing you to ! Just because some etc big man is tell you something doesn't mean that it's the truth ! Things don't really happen as they seem like ! Even Big and influential people can be misleading or incorrect , it's in human nature do mistakes and to do things which they consider at the moment to be right ,

however they may be wrong since forever and may not even know it ! Do not change your opinions just because some etc person think that you are wrong, let the time reveal the truth, stay where you are if you trust yourself and really want to fight for the truth ! Don't be a follower, be the king who is not bound anything and can stand up against anything for the justice. Still Strange and meaningless thoughts and ideas keep wandering in this world because people like to imitate each other. Nobody is ever able to tell their own real opinion. Herd mentality is what they have !

No matter how hard the world tries to cover the truth it will still remain and will come forward one day or another, that is for sure !

That's why you must have faith in yourself and should say your opinion, with confidence even if no one supports you, people will change with time when they will see the right in you, you just have to wait for your time !

Measures in simple sentences -

What is the real matter with the people, they move in herds mindlessly, if they say something today, then they will speak something else tomorrow and the day after tomorrow they will start praising someone else. You should not change your opinions, because maybe the one who is teaching you to change your opinion may not even have a opinion of their own. If you are right, then one day people will understand you, when people will feel your pain, when they will see that you were speaking about right thing then they will start supporting you eventually, all it takes is time !

कखगघङ
चछजझञ
टठडढण
तथदधन

TWELFTH NEETI

शषसह
यरलव
पफबभम

There is no greater
weapon than making your
enemy inadvertent.
Hence To win the war
In the war period,
assure the enemy
that in reality he is
winning the game
and when he will
Gets relaxed,
When His hunger
to fight subsides
Then Attack him and
erase him forever.

In this policy, Acharya Chanakya wants to tell us that Do not use your most important and powerful weapon in the first round of the war, save it for the end, keep your cards hidden until the right time arrives ! First try to confuse your enemy with the illusion that your enemy is winning the war and when his hunger to win the war subsides that is, as soon as he becomes ignorant thinking that he is going to win this war, then take out your weapons at that moment. And defeat your enemy.
Have the element of surprise !
Because that last blow should be such
Which will shatter your enemy completely !
He must not ever know your final move or your real status that whether you are winning or loosing
Keep them in illusion till the end !
Because your final bet will determine whether you will win or will be defeated in the battle.

Measures in simple sentences -

Man should hide his position whether he is winning or losing , till the last moment and do not let his enemy know his position in any situation.
Even if you are winning, still put the enemy in the illusion that you are losing.
This will make your enemy relaxed and somewhere he will definitely make a mistake.
And then in the final stage of war, when the time will come for the last blow
then use your powerful weapon, use your force, your trick which you kept hidden.

कखगघङ
चछजझञ
टठडढण
तथदधन

THIRTEENTH NEETI

शषसह
यरलव
पफबभम

When a human is
under stress,
Anxiety occurs.
At that time his mind
is also in doubt.
In times like these
One Can play with his
brain, his intelligence.
Your thoughts can be
placed on it.

When a man is tensed, confused then his mind is also skeptical. This is the time when any seed can be sown in that unstable mind

You just have to place that thought, that seed of doubt, the rest it will do on it's own

When a person is confident you can never break his thinking then but when he is already in doubt and is stressed it is the right time to manipulate him, in such a way that he becomes the reason for his own downfall himself !

Why is this possible ?

This is possible because when a person is in a lot of anxiety, his thinking ability

Will not working properly.

A person entangled in problems simply wants to get out of the problems in any way possible and for this his mind sometimes forcibly forces him to turn towards the wrong paths without him even knowing about it consciously.

But

you should also keep this in mind that it may happen that your opponents may take advantage of this and try to mislead you when you are worried. That is why it is very important that whenever you are in any concern and your brain is unable to think properly, about any solution.

So never to go to such people at that time, who are your enemies because at that time if they will sow the seed of doubt in your mind, then that seed won't

take long to grow into a full grown tree and to destroy your flower bed.

Measures in simple sentences -

Whenever man is in doubt, whenever he is
worried, when he does not see any path, any
option. Then he should settle down for some time.
And should give rest to his brain for a while
rather than taking wrong decisions in a heist !
Seeds of anxiety even a small seed can also affect
your ability to think and to understand.
That is why you should not take any decision
When you are worried also should not tell your
problems to others. Yes, it is good for the mind, to
tell it's own problems to others and to feel relieved
for some time but in reality, when you have to
decide, it is not right to say your problems on a
loud speaker for everyone to enjoy it Because you
don't really know who's your real enemy, waiting
for you to cry, thinking to make his next plan out
of your current problem, against you !
Waiting for you to tell him your weaknesses
Every wall is thin, your secrets and your problems
won't just stay with a single person, they will
reach even to the ears of those whom you would
have never even herd about that they existed !
And because you have to make
all the decisions by yourself.
So you must learn to think calmly.
Stabilise your mind.
Focus and then take the required decision by
looking at it from every possible point of view .

A disciple pays tribute to
Acharya Chanakya.

" Guru Brahma.
Guru Vishnu
Guru Devo Maheshwaraha
Guru Saakshat Para Brahma
Tasmai Sree Gurave Namaha "

Meaning -

Guru is verily the representative of Brahma,
Vishnu and Shiva. He creates, sustains
knowledge and destroys the weeds of
ignorance. I salute such a Guru.

— — — — — — — — — — — — — — — — —

YouTube channel - IT'S SIMPLE - Priyanka
Instagram id -   @itssimplepriyanka
Facebook page -   @itssimplepriyanka
Twitter -   @itssimplepri